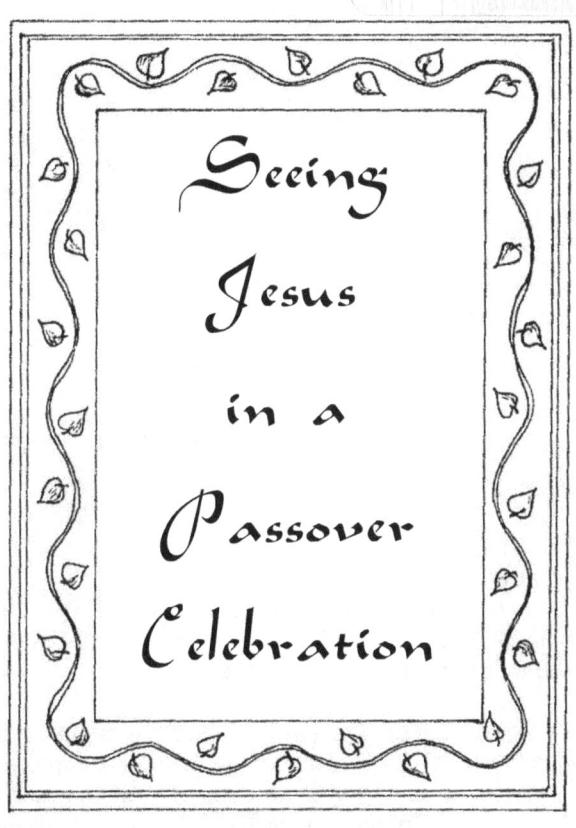

Seeing Jesus in a Passover Celebration

David W. and Jennifer L. Shorten

Text © 1996, 1998, 2012
David W. and Jennifer L. Shorten
ISBN-13: 978-0615721248

Illustrations © 1996
Jennifer L. Shorten

Scripture taken from the HOLY BIBLE,
NEW INTERNATIONAL VERSION
Copyright © 1973, 1978, 1984 International Bible Society.
Used by permission of Zondervan Bible Publishers

Please note that words referring to God are capitalized. This is the authors' preference and in some Scripture verses may be contrary to the publishing style of the original publishers.

The purpose of this Passover celebration is to increase our understanding of the prophetic death and resurrection of Jesus Christ. We the authors believe that observation of Passover is not required, but does enhance the Resurrection season.

Read aloud the *Seder* text, with the exception of directions in parentheses. For more complete instruction on hosting a *Seder* using this booklet, please refer to "Seeing Jesus in a Passover Celebration, Preparation Guide."

Luke 22:7-20

Then came the day of Unleavened Bread on which the Passover lamb had to be sacrificed. Jesus sent Peter and John, saying, "Go and make preparations for us to eat the Passover."

"Where do You want us to prepare for it?" they asked.

He replied, "As you enter the city, a man carrying a jar of water will meet you. Follow him to the house that he enters, and say to the owner of the house, 'The Teacher asks: Where is the guest room, where I may eat the Passover with my disciples?' He will show you a large upper room, all furnished. Make preparations there."

They left and found things just as Jesus had told them. So they prepared the Passover.

When the hour came, Jesus and His apostles reclined at the table. And He said to them, "I have eagerly desired to eat this Passover with you before I suffer. For I tell you, I will not eat it again until it finds fulfillment in the kingdom of God."

After taking the cup, He gave thanks and said, "Take this and divide it among you. For I tell you I will not drink again of the fruit of the vine until the kingdom of God comes."

And He took bread, gave thanks and broke it, and gave it to them, saying, "This is My body given; do this in remembrance of Me."

In the same way, after the supper He took the cup, saying, "This cup is the new covenant in My blood, which is poured out for you."

Passover

Passover commemorates the redemption of the Hebrews from Egyptian slavery. On the first Passover, each Hebrew household sacrificed a perfect yearling lamb and sprinkled its blood on the crosspiece and side posts of the door. The "Angel of Death" passed over the houses that were protected by the blood of the lamb. Where there was no blood, the first born male was slain. We are redeemed and set free by the blood of Jesus, the pure and spotless Lamb of God.

> *"For you know that it was not with perishable things such as gold or silver that you were redeemed... but with the precious blood of Christ, a lamb without blemish or defect."*
>
> *1 Peter 1:18 & 19*

As we review the Passover story, we will highlight traditional practices of a Passover *Seder*. We will also study the significance of those traditions in the lives of born-again Christians.

Introduction

The table is now prepared for the Passover Seder, or service. Notice the candles, the grape juice, the *matzah*, and the Seder Plate containing several different items. Each of these things serves a special purpose in tonight's service. The significance of each will be explained throughout the evening.

We will drink from our cups only four times tonight. With each sip, we celebrate God's promised deliverance for ancient Hebrews and how that promise relates to born-again Christians. These four promises are found in Exodus 6: 6 & 7.

A sip from the Cup of Sanctification
> *"I will bring you out from under the yoke of the Egyptians"*

A sip from the Cup of Plagues
> *"I will free you from being slaves"*

A sip from the Cup of Redemption
> *"I will redeem you with an outstretched arm"*

A sip from the Cup of Praise
> *"I will take you as My own people and I will be your God"*

Candle Lighting

> *"I am the Light of the World. Whoever follows Me will never walk in darkness, but will have the light of life."*
>
> *John 8:12*

We begin by lighting candles and praying for Jesus to be Lord of this service. The candles are lit by a woman to remind us that our Redeemer was the promised seed of a woman.

> *"I will put enmity between you and the woman, and between your offspring and hers; He will crush your head, and you will strike His heel."*
>
> *Genesis 3:15*

(Please join in prayer as candles are lit)

Cup of Sanctification

A Jewish household is symbolically set apart for Passover by the removal of leaven from the house. Even the smallest particles of leaven are swept with a feather onto a wooden spoon.

This represents the Holy Spirit guiding sinners to repentance. The Holy Spirit is often symbolized as a dove, which has feathers. Jesus was crucified on a wooden cross. The sin in our hearts is removed when we accept forgiveness through the death and shed blood of Jesus. The conviction of the Holy Spirit is able to bring even the slightest sin to obedience to God.

> *"For seven days you are to eat bread made without yeast. On the first day remove the yeast from your houses, for whoever eats anything with yeast in it from the first day through the seventh must be cut off from Israel."*
>
> *Exodus 12:15*

We share this cup tonight knowing the leaven represents sin. This "leaven" has been cleansed from our hearts through the death and shed blood of Jesus. We are sanctified, set apart for His service.

As we prepare to drink from this cup, let us thank God for setting us apart. At the Last Supper, His final Passover *Seder*, Jesus shared this cup with His disciples, saying:

> *"Take this and divide it among you. For I tell you I will not drink again of the fruit of the vine until the kingdom of God comes."*
>
> Luke 22:17 & 18

(Please join in prayer at this time)

Now let us drink for the first time from our cups.

Foot Washing

People used to walk for days before reaching Jerusalem to celebrate Passover. When they arrived at the feast location, their feet were calloused and caked with dirt. A humble servant washed and dried each person's feet, scrubbing away the filth of the journey.

While Jesus' disciples argued over which of them was the greatest, Jesus took off His outer clothes and picked up a towel.

> *"After that, He poured water into a basin and began to wash His disciples' feet, drying them with the towel that was wrapped around Him."*
>
> *John 13:5*

In this manner, Jesus reinforced His teachings that we are to serve one another and consider others better than ourselves.

Since foot washing is very time-consuming, it is often omitted from a Passover Service. Sometimes, hands are symbolically washed instead.

Jewish households may use a two-handled ritual wash cup and a basin for this ceremony. The *Seder* leader pours water onto his hands over the basin. He first pours the water twice onto his right hand and then twice onto his left hand. He dries his hands on nearby towel (traditionally held by a child) before his hostess removes the wash cup, basin and towel.

(Leader demonstrates and/or briefly describes method for washing one another's feet or hands, as desired)

Karpas

Passover is celebrated in the Spring, when the earth is in bloom with new life. (Leader lifts parsley or other herb) This herb represents new life. (Leader lifts salt water) Salt water represents tears shed by the Hebrews. Their tears were caused by the bondage of slavery in Egypt.

Those who have accepted Jesus as Savior recognize that new life in Christ is often marred by tears. These tears are caused by the pain and suffering of bondage to sin.

> *"Dear friends, do not be surprised at the painful trial you are suffering, as though something strange were happening to you. But rejoice that you participate in the sufferings of Christ, so that you may be overjoyed when His glory is revealed."*
>
> *1 Peter 4:12 & 13*

As each of us dips a sprig of herbs into salt water, we remember suffering both in the lives of the Hebrew slaves and in our own lives. At the same time, we rejoice that the lives of sinners are made new through Jesus.

(Please join in prayer at this time)

Now let us dip a piece of herb in salt water and eat the herbs together.

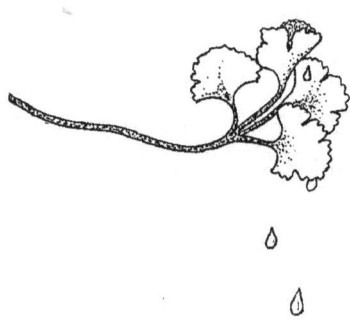

Four Questions

"And when your children ask you, 'What does this ceremony mean to you?' then tell them, 'It is the Passover of the L<small>ORD</small>...'"
Exodus 12:26

At this time, a young child would ask four standard questions:

> Why during a Passover meal do we only eat *matzah* and not other bread?
>
> Why during a Passover meal do we only eat bitter herbs and not other vegetables?
>
> Why do we dip our vegetables twice during a Passover meal?
>
> Why do we relax and enjoy the Passover meal when the Hebrews ate it in haste?

We will reflect on each question from our Christian perspective.

Matzah

During a Passover meal, only *matzah* bread is eaten. When the Israelites left Egypt, they took with them bread made without yeast. God had instructed that yeast be left out of the dough because there would be no time for the dough to rise.

The Bible likens yeast to sin:

> *"Don't you know that a little yeast works through the whole dough? Get rid of the old yeast that you may be a new batch without yeast - as you really are."*
>
> 1 Corinthians 5:7

For both Jews and Christians, Passover is a time to determine to rid oneself of sinful habits. It is a time to begin a new life which is glorifying to the Lord.

(Leader places three *matzot* in a *matzah tash* or napkin)
Three *matzot* are wrapped together for Passover. Some ancient Hebrews speculated this to represent unity of the Patriarchs - Abraham, Isaac and Jacob. Others have determined it to symbolize unity of the congregation - priests, temple-workers and worshipers. Christians quickly recognize the unity of God - Father, Son and Holy Spirit.

For more than 1500 years before Jesus was crucified, the Jewish people would remove the center piece of matzah and break it in half. This tradition is still continued today, although many people do not understand its significance.

The prophet Isaiah wrote about the Messiah:

> *"Surely He took up our infirmities and carried our sorrows, yet we considered Him stricken by God, smitten by Him, and afflicted."*
>
> *Isaiah 53:4*

We can view the stack of three *matzot* as representing the Trinity. The center piece of *matzah* represents the Son, Jesus. This piece is removed from the others and broken, just as Jesus was removed from God the Father and the Holy Spirit and was crucified. (Leader removes center piece of matzah and breaks it in half)

One piece of this broken *matzah* is wrapped and hidden. (Leader wraps *afikomen* in napkin or bag and hides it) The *matzah* that is hidden reminds us that the body of Jesus was also wrapped and hidden - in a tomb. This *afikomen* is later returned for the completion of the meal, reminding us that Jesus also returned - from the dead.

Break off a piece of unleavened bread, or *matzah*. As we prepare to eat it together, remember that the removal of yeast from the bread symbolizes the removal of sin from our lives.

(Please join in prayer at this time)

Now let us eat this *matzah* together.

Bitter Herbs

The second question asks about the bitter herbs which are served. (Leader lifts horseradish) This horseradish reminds us of the bitter lives of enslaved Hebrews. It also reminds Christians of the bitterness of a life enslaved to sin.

> *"But the more they were oppressed, the more they multiplied and spread; so the Egyptians came to dread the Israelites and worked them ruthlessly. They made their lives bitter with hard labor in brick and mortar and with all kinds of work in the fields."*
>
> *Exodus 1:12 - 14*

The third question asks why we dip vegetables twice during a Passover *Seder*. We dipped one herb in salt water. This time dip lettuce into the horseradish.

(Please join in prayer at this time)

Now let us eat the bitter herbs together.

Kharoset

(Leader lifts *kharoset*) This mixture of apples, honey and nuts is called *kharoset*. Scoop some horseradish onto a piece of *matzah*. Scoop *kharoset* onto a second piece of *matzah* and place the items together to form a "sandwich." *Kharoset* with horseradish represents the sweet hope God brings to even the most bitter lives.

> *"We also rejoice in our sufferings, because we know that suffering produces perseverance; perseverance, character; and character, hope."*
>
> *Romans 5:3 & 4*

(Please join in prayer at this time)

Now let us eat the *kharoset* together.

Reclining

"He who dwells in the shelter of the Most High will rest in the shadow of the Almighty."

Psalm 91:1

The final question asks about reclining, or resting during the Passover meal.

The first Passover was eaten quickly by people preparing to leave their lives of slavery in Egypt. Today, Jewish people recline during a Passover meal because they are not slaves in Egypt.

As people set free from the bondage of sin, Christians relax and enjoy the Passover meal.

The Passover Story

"The month is to be for you the first month, the first month of your year. Tell the whole community of Israel that on the tenth day of this month each man is to take a lamb for his family, one for each household...

"The animals you choose must be year-old males without defect, and you may take them from the sheep or the goats. Take care of them until the fourteenth day of the month, when all the people of the community of Israel must slaughter them at twilight. Then they are to take some of the blood and put it on the sides and tops of the door frames of the houses where they eat the lambs. That same night they are to eat the meat roasted over the fire, along with bitter herbs, and bread made without yeast...

"This is how you are to eat it: with your cloak tucked into your belt, your sandals on your feet and your staff in your hand. Eat it in haste; it is the Lord's Passover. On that same night I will pass through Egypt and strike down every firstborn - both men and animals - and I will bring judgment on all the gods of Egypt. I am the Lord. The blood will be a sign for you on the houses where you are; and when I see the blood, I will pass over you."

Exodus 12:2, 3, 5-8, 11-13

The Sacrifice Lamb

"The next day John saw Jesus coming toward Him and said, 'Look, the Lamb of God, who takes away the sin of the world.'"

John 1:29

God commanded the Israelites to sacrifice lambs. The people had four days to inspect their lambs and ensure the lambs' perfection. Jesus was under close scrutiny by the scribes and religious leaders during His four days in Jerusalem. In an act of hypocrisy, they denied Jesus' perfection. Jesus was handed over on the fourteenth day of the month to be crucified.

God brought darkness to the land for three hours when His Son died, reflecting the twilight hour of sacrifice.

The Passover tray no longer contains lamb, but only a dry bone. Jewish homes omit lamb because there is no temple in Jerusalem for sacrificing.

Christians recognize Jesus as the sacrificed lamb, and need no other lamb. The bone remains to remind us how dry and lifeless we are without Jesus.

Focus again on the Passover tray. A hard-boiled egg has replaced the lamb. For Jewish people who do not accept Jesus as their Messiah, the egg is a symbol of mourning. The people mourn because there is no longer a temple where they can sacrifice.

For all who accept Jesus as the Messiah, the egg is a symbol of new life in Christ. The round shape of the egg, which has no beginning or ending, reminds us also of the anticipation of eternal life.

> *"For the L*ORD *Himself will come down from heaven, with a loud command, with the voice of the archangel and with the trumpet call of God, and the dead in Christ will rise first. After that, we who are left will be caught up with them in the clouds to meet the L*ORD *in the air. And so we will be with the L*ORD *forever."*
>
> *1 Thessalonians 4:16 & 17*

Cup of Plagues

Along with instructions for preparing the Passover lamb, God revealed to Moses:

> *"On the same night I will pass through Egypt and strike down every firstborn - both men and animals - and I will bring judgment on all the gods of Egypt; I am the L<small>ORD</small>."*
> *Exodus 12:12*

The plagues God sent to afflict the Egyptians caused pain, suffering and bloodshed in their lives.

Carefully dip a corner of your napkin into your cup. The stain of juice symbolizes the blood shed by the Egyptians during the plagues of blood, frogs, gnats, flies, cattle disease, boils, hail, locusts, darkness and death of the firstborn.

The full cup of juice, which represents fullness of joy, has been diminished because of the sorrow caused by the plagues.

For the escaping slaves, the plagues had different significance. To them, the plagues symbolized God's perseverance on behalf of His people. With great joy, the Israelites celebrated when God had taken them safely to the far bank of the Red Sea.

Believers in Christ have also moved from a place of slavery to a place of safety. We did not have to cross the Red Sea; instead Jesus revealed:

> *"I am the Gate; whoever enters through Me will be saved."*
>
> *John 10:9*

(Please join in prayer at this time)

Remembering the joy of salvation, let us now drink for the second time from our cups.

The Passover Meal

A "traditional" Passover meal varies greatly from family to family. Time-honored dishes such as *matzah* ball soup and *gefilte* fish may be accompanied by a variety of fresh vegetables. Coconut macaroons or ice cream are sometimes offered for dessert, since many other sweets contain a leavening agent.

(If serving a meal, leader should relate any necessary information at this time. If the meal is omitted, continue with the following optional text)

A traditional Passover *Seder* includes a full holiday meal at this time. For ease in conducting this service, we chose to eliminate the meal. Instead we will now continue with the service.

Afikomen

Earlier in tonight's service we removed the center piece of *matzah*, which represents the Son of God. That *matzah* was broken, wrapped and hidden.

The Passover Celebration cannot be completed without the return of the *afikomen*. In a traditional Jewish service the children are sent to search for the *afikomen* at this time. When it is found, it is redeemed by the service leader for a small amount of money.

We now begin the most sacred part of the Passover *Seder* - sharing the *afikomen* and the third cup. This is what is widely recognized as the Lord's Supper, or Holy Communion.

> *"A man ought to examine himself before he eats of the bread and drinks of the cup. For anyone who eats and drinks without recognizing the body of the Lord eats and drinks judgment on himself."*
>
> 1 Corinthians 11:28 & 29

Let us all take time to examine ourselves. Anyone needing to be reconciled with God or with another person may ask forgiveness at this time. If anyone here does not have a personal relationship with Jesus, we ask that you not participate in the Lord's Supper.

If you would like to take the Lord's Supper and you are not sure you are saved, please talk with a person sitting near you. They will direct you to someone with whom you can talk at this time.

(Please pause for personal reflection while the leader retrieves the *afikomen* or sends children to search for it)

In the *matzah*, we can see reminders of Jesus, the Messiah. Hold a piece of *matzah* and notice the stripes in it.

> *"But He was wounded for our transgressions, He was bruised for our iniquities; the chastisement of our peace was upon Him, and with His stripes we are healed."*
>
> Isaiah 53:5

Now lift the *matzah* up toward the light. Notice that the *matzah* is pierced.

> *"I will pour upon the house of David, and upon the inhabitants of Jerusalem, the spirit of grace and of supplications: and they shall look upon Me whom they have pierced, and they shall mourn for Him as one mourns for his only son."*
> Zechariah 12:10

At this time during the Last Supper, Jesus took the *afikomen*, broke it, and gave thanks to God.

(Please join in prayer at this time)

Jesus then revealed:

> *"This is My body given for you; do this in remembrance of Me."*
>
> Luke 22:19

Just as the *afikomen* has returned to complete the Passover meal, Jesus returned to life.

> *"Why do you look for the living among the dead? He is not here; He has risen!"*
>
> Luke 24:5b - 6a

Now let us eat this *matzah* together, remembering the body of the Lamb of God, who takes away the sins of the world.

Cup of Redemption

This is the cup "after supper" during which we remember that God saved, or redeemed, the Hebrews from slavery. More importantly, He redeemed us from eternity in hell. Jesus lifted up this cup and said:

> *"This cup is the new covenant in My blood which is poured out for you."*
>
> *Luke 22:20*

The blood of a sacrificed lamb on the door was a sign to the Angel of Death to pass over that household, leaving the inhabitants unharmed. The blood of the Lamb of God on our hearts prevents death from claiming victory over Christians.

(Please join in prayer at this time)

Now let us drink together from the Cup of Redemption.

Elijah the Prophet

Some Talmudic scholars believe a fifth promise is found in Exodus 6, necessitating a fifth cup.

> *"And I will bring you into the land I swore with uplifted hand to give to Abraham, to Isaac and to Jacob. I will give it to you as a possession. I am the Lord."*
>
> *Exodus 6:8*

Other scholars argue that this promise was fulfilled when Joshua led the Hebrews into the Promised Land.

Peaceful compromise is reached in a fifth cup being filled, but not drunk. This fifth cup is named in honor of *Eliyahu HaNavi*, Elijah the Prophet, who did not die.

> *"As they were walking along and talking together, suddenly a chariot of fire and horses of fire appeared and separated the two of them, and Elijah went up to heaven in a whirlwind."*
>
> *2 Kings 2:11*

Many Jewish people still look for the return of Elijah.

> *"See, I will send you the prophet Elijah before that great and dreadful day of the Lord comes."*
>
> Malachi 4:5

Christians believe John the Baptist came in the spirit and power of Elijah (see Luke 1:17). Jesus said of John the Baptist:

> *"And if you are willing to accept it, he is the Elijah who was to come."*
>
> Matthew 11:14

It is generally believed that Elijah will answer all queries upon his return. This includes settling the issue of how many cups to drink at a Passover *Seder*.

Cup of Praise

Before our Passover meal is complete, we will drink one final time from our cups.

Drinking from this Cup of Praise is not only a singular act of praising God for His goodness. It is also a pledge of committing our lives to the Lord.

> *"Glorify the Lord with me; let us exalt His Name together."*
>
> Psalm 34:3

(Please join in prayer at this time)

Now let us finish drinking from our cups as we prepare to glorify the God in song.

In Conclusion

The teaching of the Passover *Seder* is complete. The traditional refrain, "Next year in Jerusalem" is repeated each year by people who look forward to returning to their native land.

Those of us who know Jesus as our Lord and Savior anticipate spending eternity in heaven with Him. We proclaim together:

Next year in the New Jerusalem!

We are now ready for a time of celebration. Please join in praise and worship of the resurrected Lamb of God.

(Conclude the service with a time of celebration in song)

www.ingramcontent.com/pod-product-compliance
Lightning Source LLC
Chambersburg PA
CBHW051705040426
42446CB00009B/1317